BAD FOR GOOD CHILDREN

by

Brian Wilks

Published in 2003 by: Hopscotch Educational Publishing Ltd, Unit 2, The Old Brushworks, 56 Pickwick Road, Corsham, Wiltshire, SN13 9BX

Tel: 01249 701701

© Brian Wilks

Written by Brian Wilks
Series design by Blade Communications
Cover illustration by Susan Hutchison
Illustrated by Susan Hutchison and the pupils of St Agnes' PNEU School
Printed by Athenaeum Press, Gateshead

ISBN 1-904307-43-4

Brian Wilks hereby asserts his moral right to be identified as the author of this work in accordance with the Copyright, Designs and Patents Act, 1988.

All rights reserved. This book is sold subject to the condition that it shall not, by way of trade or otherwise, be lent, hired out or otherwise circulated without the publisher's prior consent in any form of binding or cover other than that in which it is published and without a similar condition, including this condition, being imposed upon the subsequent purchaser.

No part of this publication may be reproduced, stored in a retrieval system, or transmitted, in any form or by any means, electronic, mechanical, photocopying, recording or otherwise, without the prior permission of the publisher.

To Tessa and Zak

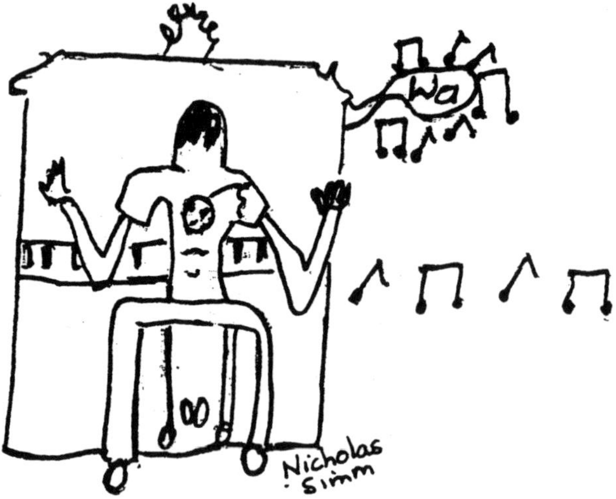
Wa
Nicholas Simm

If you have a sister Anna
Why not put her in the piano?
Then practising the minor scales
Would be accompanied by wails.

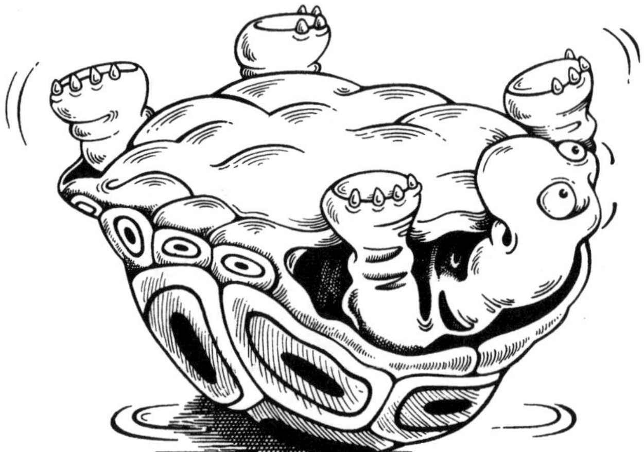

If your tortoise should turn turtle,
Turning turtle tortoise do,
Simply turn the tortoise turtle
Then it will be pleased with you.

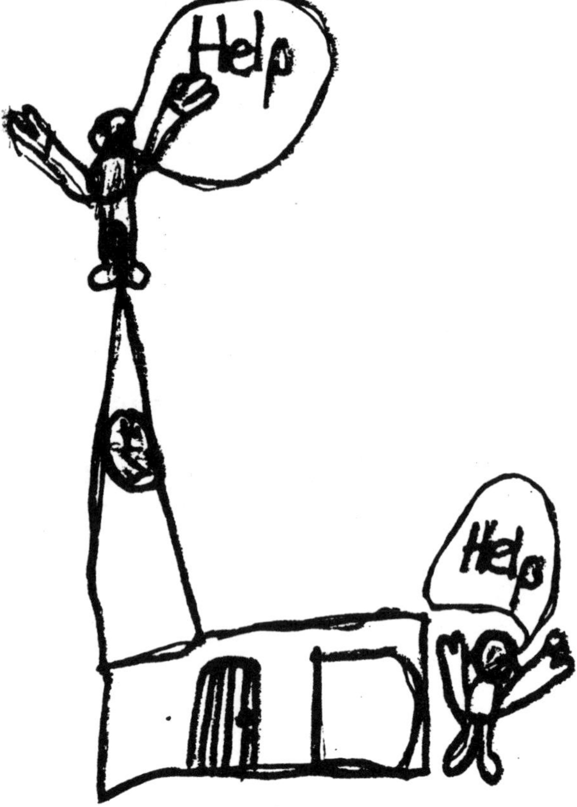
Help
Help

BAD POEMS FOR GOOD CHILDREN

Have you thought how many people
Could perch upon a high steeple
Or better still how many fall
Before they reach the top at all?

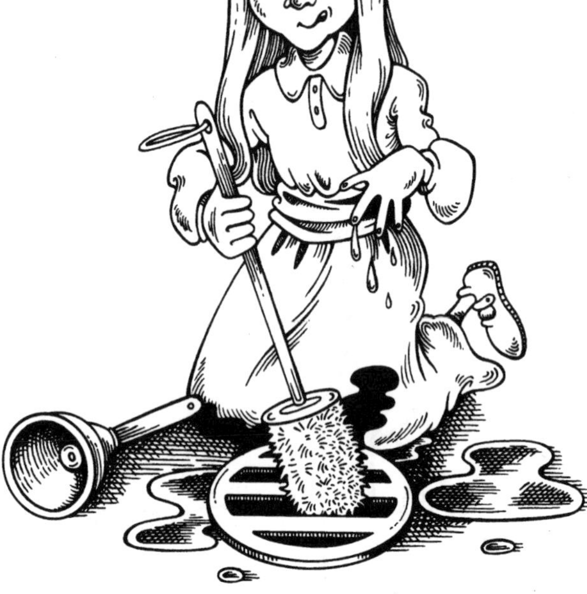

When your clothes are stiff and new
Your mother would be pleased with
    you
If you cleaned a dirty drain
Or took apart a cycle chain.

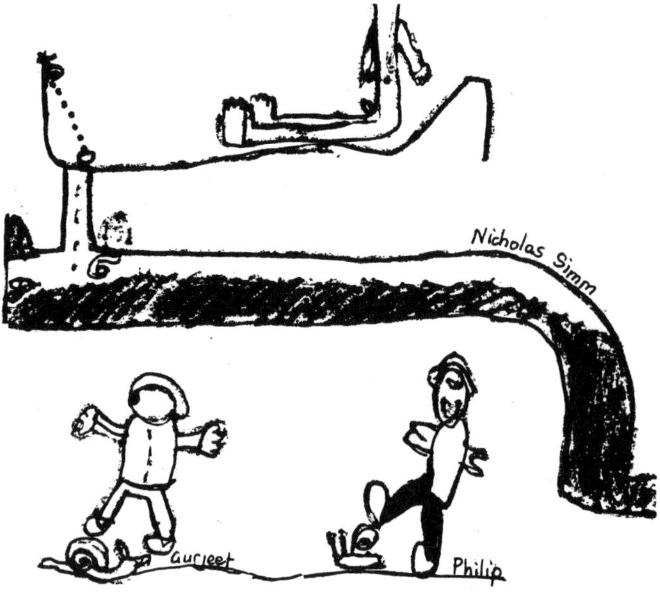
Nicholas Simm
Gurjeet
Philip

Should a snail cross your path
Put it in your brother's bath.
If you stamp upon it well
The plug will take it, slime and shell.

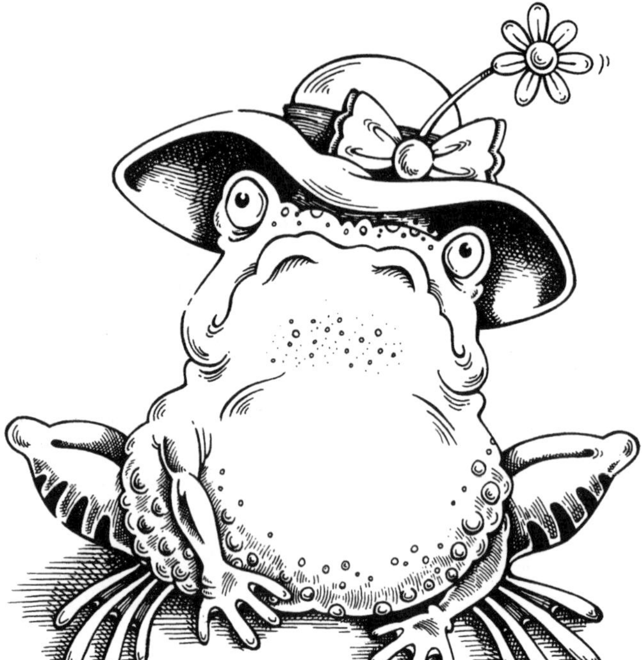

Frogs and newts and worms and bats
Are picturesque in mother's hats.
While anything with claws or flippers
Goes very well in father's slippers.

Jolyon

Nothing pleases mothers more
Than food that's trodden in the floor.
And fathers too are pleased to see
Their daily papers soaked in tea.

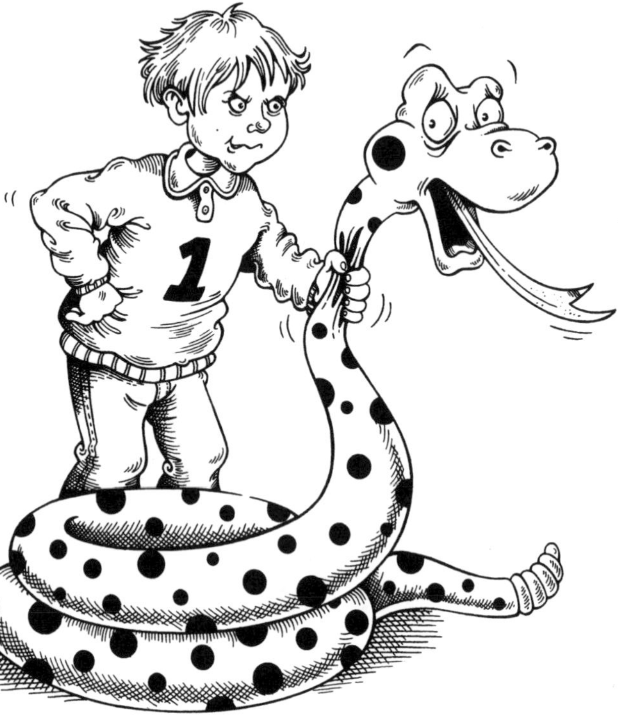

If a sleeping snake you find
Grab it quickly from behind.
Then with a sudden yell of warning
Throw it in a tent or awning.

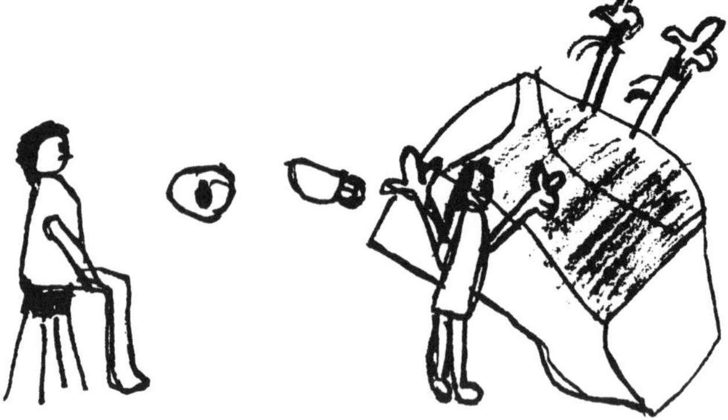

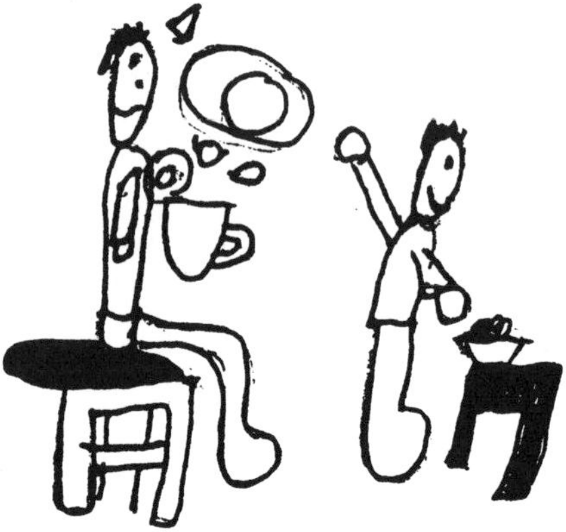

If your brother is a fool
Why not place him on a stool
And fling at him a plate or cup
While you do the washing up.

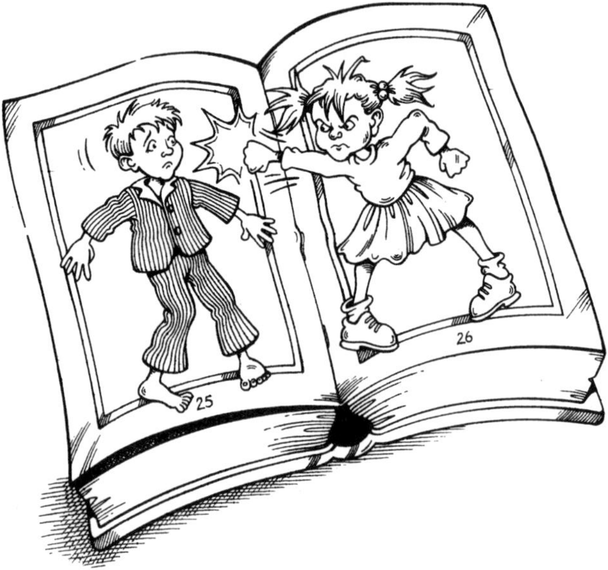
25
26

Someone in a book I read
Said he would not go to bed.
So someone in an awful rage
Hit him on another page.

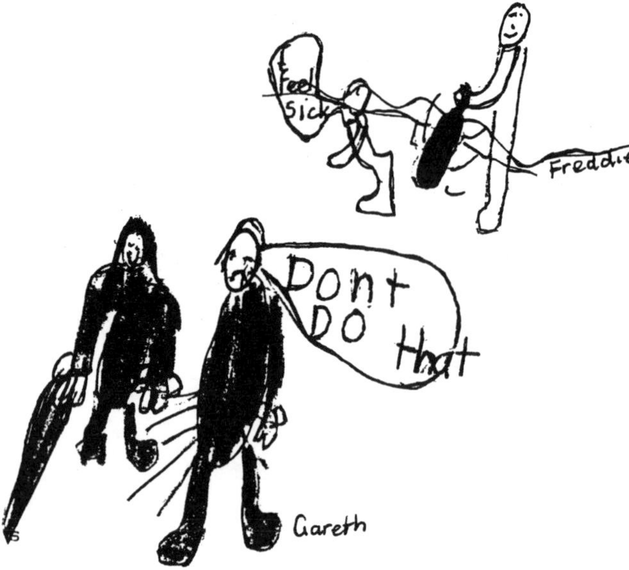
Feel Sick
Freddie
Dont DO that
Gareth

The mother of a boy who's bad
Will often be extremely glad
If you should beat him with a stick
Until he says he's feeling sick.

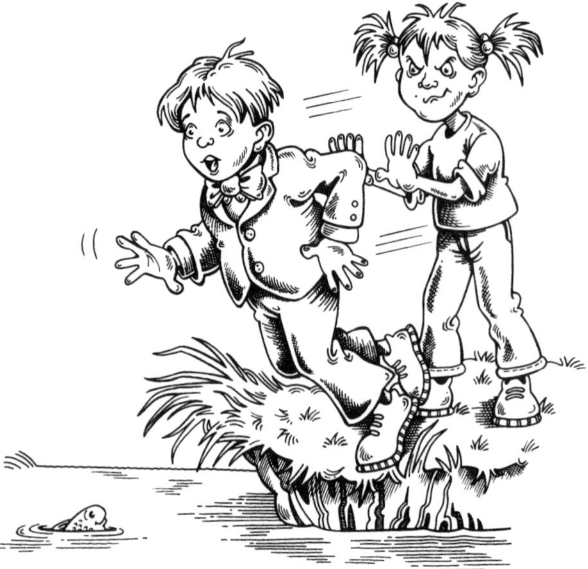

If of rich cousins you're not fond
Why not push them in the pond?
A single satisfying splosh
Will warn them not to be so posh.

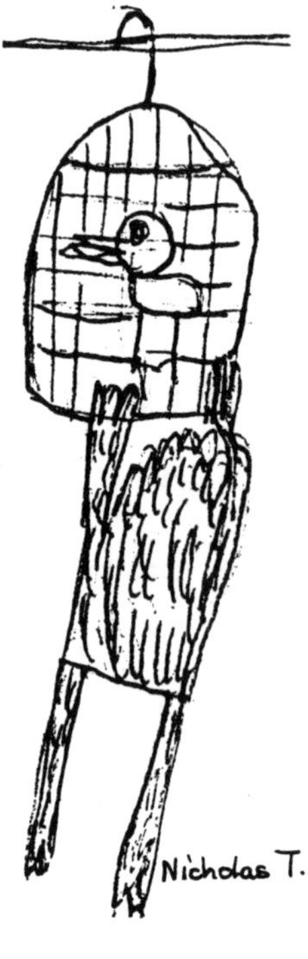
Nicholas T.

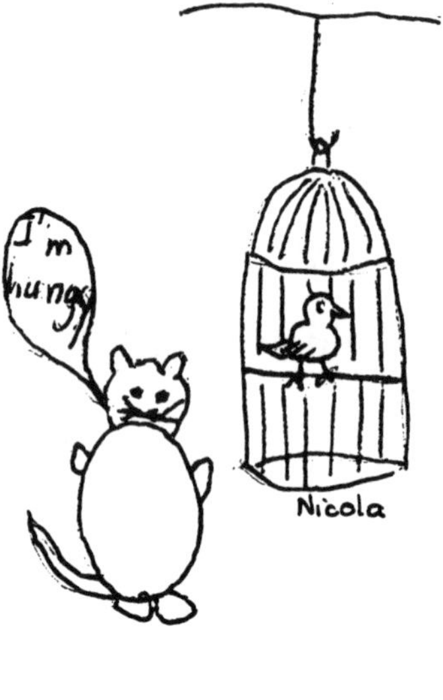
I'm
hungry
Nicola

Aunties who keep birds in cages
Will have the most delightful rages
If you show their gentle kitten
That those birds taste nice once bitten.

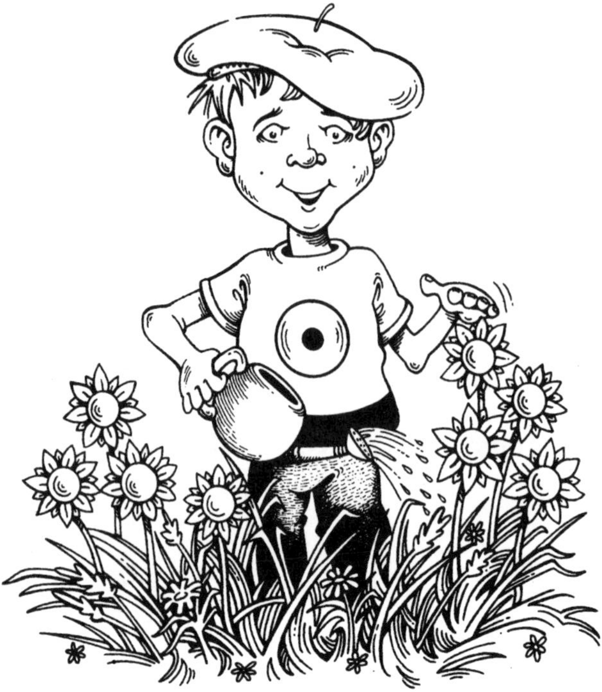

If you should spot a patch of weeds
Gather up the little seeds
Sow them with those prize crysanths
That your father fetched from France.

Nicholas T.

William W.

Climb up on the wardrobe dear,
You will find the ceiling near.
Then when you are feeling ready
You can jump and flatten Freddy.

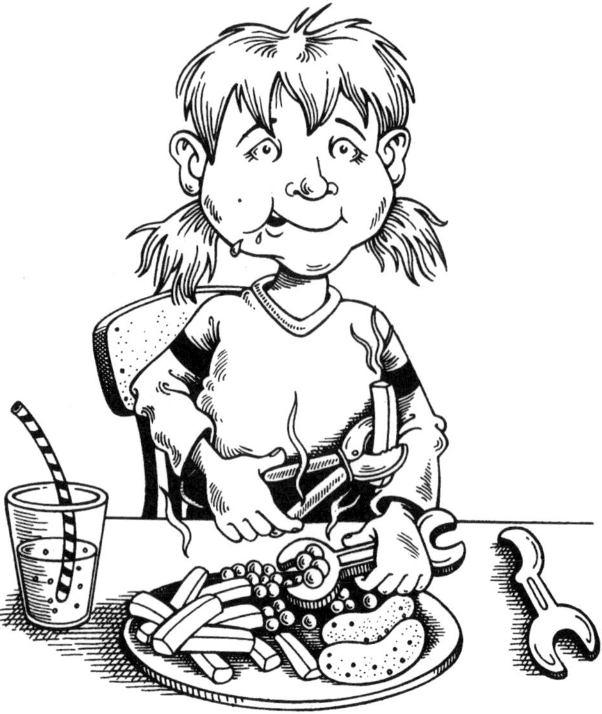

People who have proper manners
Do not eat with pliers or spanners
Nor do they mend their motor car
With fingered toast and caviar.

Joanna

If your sisters are absurd
Plaster them with lemon curd
Then shut them in the garden shed
With spiders' webs and things
they dread.

Nicholas T.

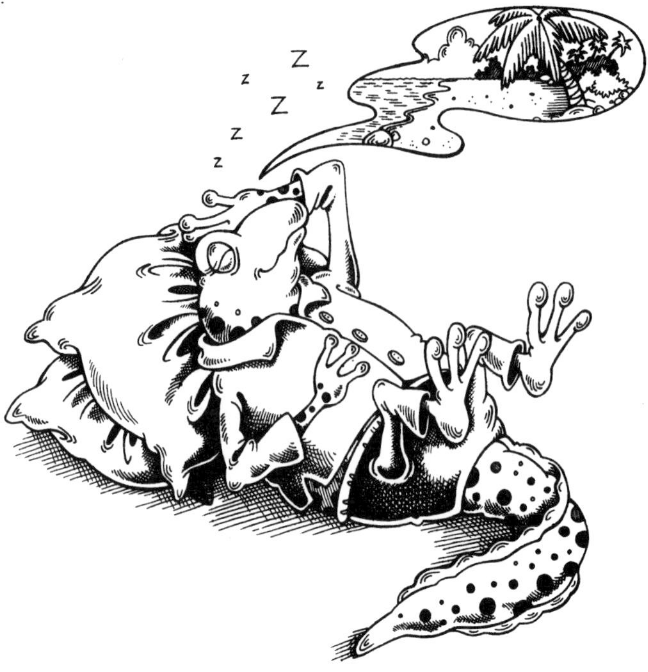
Z
z
z
Z
Z
z

Lizards from the far Bahamas
Like to sleep in clean pyjamas.
They will have the nicest dreams
While your brother screams and
    screams.

Jolyon

A mouse that's dead and in a trap

Doesn't interest me a scrap.

I'd rather let them all run free

And give them cheese and cups of tea.

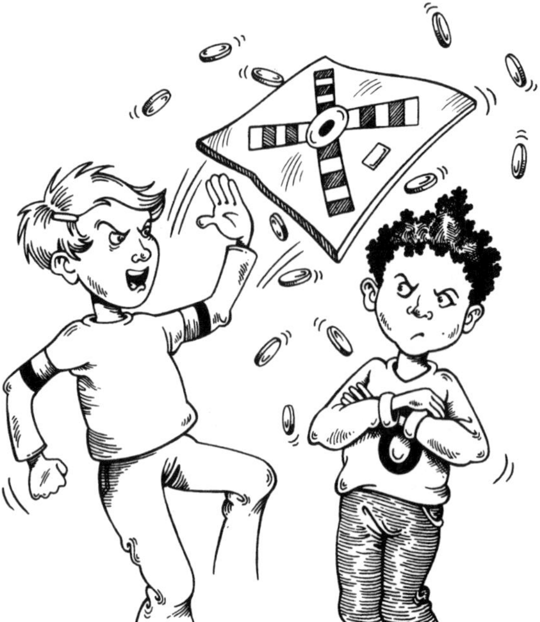

If you find a game a bore
Stamp about and slam a door.
Take two goes instead of one
Then everyone will have more fun.

Philip

Never pass a puddle by
For, when it is clear and dry
You'll realise you missed the fun
Of splattering mud on everyone.

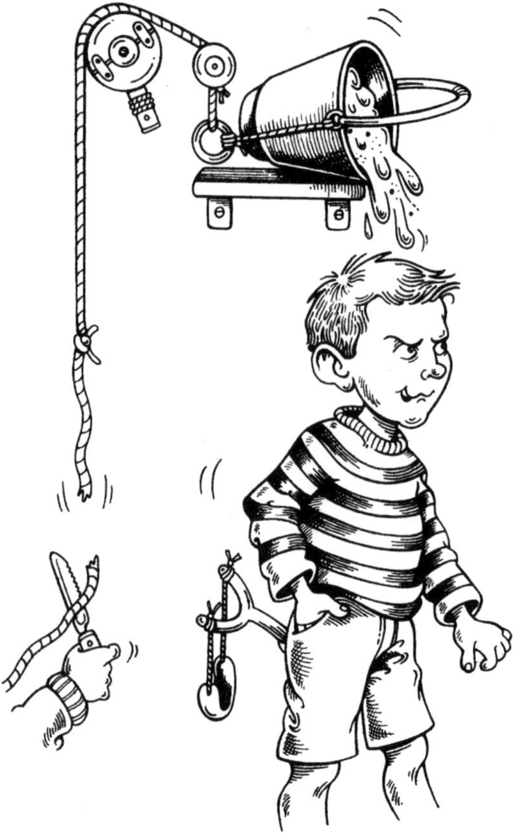

If your brother is a bully
Hoist a bucket up a pulley,
Then when he is walking by
You may let that bucket fly.